Titanic Tragedy

Jane Penrose

All Aboard!

The *Titanic* was the biggest, fastest, and finest ocean-liner of its time. In fact, it wasn't just a ship – it was more like a **floating city**! When the 270-metre luxury liner pulled out of Southampton docks on 10th April 1912, it was known as the world's first unsinkable ship. It was bound for New York, and among the 2228 passengers and crew starting out on this once-in-a-lifetime journey were 115 children. Within five days, all of these children would find themselves in the middle of a terrifying disaster in the freezing waters of the Atlantic Ocean …

As the Titanic tragedy unfolds, write down and keep your answers to each **QUIZ** question. (Remember, the answers are in the book!) Now, let's set sail!

Read on to find out what caused people to abandon ship!

Let's get ship-shape!

Step on board the amazing Titanic and take a tour.
PAGES 6 TO 7

That's Some Ship!

First-Class Finery

Explore the decks of the poshest passengers on board.
PAGES 8 TO 11

See how second class sailed!
PAGES 12 TO 15

Second-Class Citizens

Those in Third

What was life like for the poorest passengers?

PAGES 16 TO 19

Titanic Trivia

How many sausages was the Titanic carrying?

PAGES 20 TO 21

Sinkable? Unthinkable!

The Titanic struck an iceberg! Find out its fate ...

PAGES 22 TO 25

SOS!

Who came to the rescue of the Titanic's freezing survivors?

PAGES 26 TO 29

Into the Deep

Dive beneath the waves to see the Titanic as it is now ...

PAGES 30 TO 31

That's Some Ship!

Imagine a ship so large that to explore every part of it could take you at least a week! The *Titanic*'s ten decks made it the largest moving object of its time, and offered extreme luxury for its passengers on their voyage to New York (so long as they could afford it!). Passengers were separated into three classes. As well as the adults on board, there were 84 children in the *Titanic*'s poorest third class, 25 children in second class, and only 6 extra-lucky children travelling in luxurious first-class accommodation.

FiNaNCe FaCT

The *Titanic* cost £1.5 million to build in 1912. But the film *Titanic* (made in 1997) cost more than £100 million to make! Building the *Titanic* today would cost more than £200 million.

QUIZ To ******* every part of the *Titanic* coul

This advert made many people book a ticket on the **Titanic**.

First-Class Finery

THE TITANIC

First Class Passenger

SURNAME: Dodge
FIRST NAME: Washington Jnr
NATIONALITY: American
AGE: 4 years
DESTINATION: San Francisco, USA
TRAVELLING WITH: Father, Dr Washington Dodge Snr
Mother, Mrs Ruth Dodge

When Washington Dodge Jnr set foot on the *Titanic*, he was one of the luckiest boys on board. Washington had just been on a long holiday in Europe with his family, and his luck didn't stop there. He now got to travel home in luxury as one of the *Titanic's* first-class passengers. Most of the *Titanic's* top four decks were reserved for the super-rich first class, who would have paid up to £900 each for a ticket – a whopping £50,290 in today's money!

Washington's cabin would have looked like this. Check out the four-poster bed!

Washington didn't talk to the scruffs in the lower classes, as the ship was strictly divided between the 'haves' and the 'have-nots'. Second-class passengers could sometimes meet first-class passengers on deck for a game or two, but locked gates stopped anyone from third class getting near them!

First-class passengers could relax in this exotic Turkish Bath.

QUIZ When dinner was ready in first class, a trumpeter

Food Fact

The first-class passengers spent a lot of time filling their faces. Every evening they chewed their way through an 11-course dinner! A trumpeter would walk along the decks playing 'The Old Roast Beef of England', to let them know their posh nosh was ready!

So, with only six children in first class, Washington didn't have many friends to play with. Instead, he spent his time riding the gymnasium's electric camel, swimming in the pool and playing games on deck. But soon he would have more to think about than fun and games …

Second-Class Citizens

THE TITANIC

Second Class Passenger

SURNAME: Hart
FIRST NAMES: Eva Miriam
NATIONALITY: British
AGE: 7 years
DESTINATION: Winnipeg, Canada
TRAVELLING WITH: Father, Mr Benjamin Hart
Mother, Mrs Esther Hart

Being a second-class passenger on the *Titanic* was still a pretty good ticket, as Eva Hart and her parents found out. They were moving to Canada, and you can imagine how excited Eva was! However, Eva's mother wasn't excited – she was **TERRIFIED**. She had an awful feeling that something bad would happen to the *Titanic*, so she sat up every night keeping watch, and slept during the day. Eva had no such worries, and spent most of her time playing with six-year-old Nancy Harper, whom she met on board.

In second class, you didn't get a four-poster bed, but the cabins were still luxurious.

There were no organised activities for children on board the *Titanic*, so Eva and Nancy made their own fun. The second-class area had libraries, cafés, lounges and a lift between decks – plenty of places to get into trouble if you were a bored seven-year-old! While playing hide-and-seek around the kennels on F-deck, Eva made friends with an ugly old bulldog. She would visit her four-legged friend every morning, sometimes with scraps of food saved from the previous night's dinner.

FELiNE FaCT

Although there were dogs on board the *Titanic*, there were no cats. Cats were often kept on ships to keep mice away, and as good-luck mascots, so perhaps the *Titanic* could have done with one after all!

Wish you were here!

It's great fun on the decks. I love the sea air!

Those in Third

THE TITANIC

Third Class Passenger

SURNAME: Goldsmith
FIRST NAMES: Frank John William ('Frankie')
NATIONALITY: British
AGE: 9 years
DESTINATION: Detroit, USA
TRAVELLING WITH: Father, Mr Frank Goldsmith Snr
Mother, Mrs Emily Goldsmith

Nine-year-old Frankie Goldsmith was one of 84 children in third class. He and his family were sailing to America to start a new life in Detroit, and Frankie was as excited about the voyage as he was about his new life. Frankie's dad was a builder, and had saved hard to afford the family's tickets at £7 each – about £425 in today's money.

Frankie's family would have been much more cramped in their cabin than either Eva or Washington!

Although he was a third-class passenger, Frankie probably had more fun than Washington or Eva. The third-class decks were at the bottom of the ship, and Frankie and his gang of friends would hang from the baggage cranes or make dens in the ship's hold. Frankie loved to watch the soot-blackened men in the engine room, singing as they shovelled coal into the *Titanic*'s gigantic, fiery engines.

QUIZ In the engine room, men would sing as they shovelled

FieRY FaCT

The *Titanic* had 159 furnaces and 29 boilers, all fed by 825 tonnes of coal per day! An accidental fire broke out in one of the coal bunkers before the *Titanic* set sail, and was still burning during the voyage!

"Anyone would think that ship was doomed!"

Third-class passengers were encouraged to go to bed by 10 p.m., but this still left plenty of time for fun. Everyone got to know each other, and there was a lively atmosphere in the third-class dining room. At night, many of them would sing or tell stories; little did they know they themselves were about to take part in one of history's most terrifying tales …

coal into the Titanic's ✱✱✱✱✱✱✱✱, fiery engines.

Titanic Trivia

Dog overboard!
It wasn't only people who wanted to sail to New York. On board there were nine dogs, four hens, thirty cockerels and one yellow canary. Two dogs and the canary survived!

Bizarre baggage
As well as normal suitcases and trunks in the ship's hold, there was a car and a marmalade-making machine!

Fake funnel
The **Titanic** only needed three of its four funnels. The fourth was added to make the ship look more grand and powerful!

Big breakfast
There were forty thousand eggs in the **Titanic's** stores – as well as twenty thousand sausages!

Sinkable? Unthinkable!

At just before midnight, four days into the voyage, Eva's mother was awake as usual, worrying about the ship. Just then, she felt a jolt and a judder, and knew that this was her worst nightmare coming true. The *Titanic* had struck something – an iceberg – and water was flooding into the ship through a gash in the side.

> Icebergs are massive chunks of ice that have broken away from glaciers. Only the top tenth of an iceberg can be seen – the other nine-tenths are hidden underwater, which makes them really dangerous to ships.

FReaKY FaCT

Fourteen years before the *Titanic* set sail, Morgan Robertson wrote a story about the largest ship ever built hitting an iceberg in the Atlantic Ocean on a cold April night. The ship in the story was called the *Titan!*

Believing that the *Titanic* was unsinkable, many of the passengers weren't worried at first, but things soon turned serious, and first- and second-class passengers were sent up on deck. Many third-class passengers weren't told about what had happened.

Women and children were allowed on the lifeboats first, but many of the third-class passengers were stopped from getting up on deck. Washington and his parents were put into a lifeboat, as were Eva and her mother. Frankie and his mother fought their way past panicked passengers to get into the very last lifeboat. Frankie's dad patted him on the shoulder and said, "See you later".

Tragically, the Titanic didn't have enough lifeboats for everyone. For Frankie and Eva, that was the last time they ever saw their fathers.

At 2:20 a.m. on 15th April 1912... **the Titanic SANK** TO THE ICY DEPTHS OF THE ATLANTIC OCEAN.

SOS!

No one had believed that the mighty *Titanic* could sink, so no one was prepared when it did. Of the 2228 people on board, 1523 drowned. Most of them were third-class passengers who had not reached the lifeboats in time, and men who had let women and children take the places on the few lifeboats there were. So what happened to Washington, Eva and Frankie?

People in the lifeboats rowed away from the *Titanic*, hoping that another ship would rescue those left on board. Many still didn't believe that the *Titanic* would sink.

FReeZiNG FaCT

The water in the North Atlantic Ocean was so cold that no one could have survived in it for longer than 15 minutes.

Washington was in lifeboat 5, wearing only his pyjamas as the lifeboat bobbed past the icebergs in the Atlantic Ocean. Eva Hart was in lifeboat 14, wrapped up in a blanket. She was sick with pain from hitting her stomach on the side of the lifeboat when she was thrown in. As for Frankie Goldsmith, his mother covered his eyes as their lifeboat rowed away from the sinking ship. All three were **lucky to be alive**, but were still cold and frightened, stuck in the middle of a freezing sea in tiny boats. **What could they do?**

QUIZ The Titanic's passengers were rescued b

Before the *Titanic* sank, its crew had sent the message SOS (meaning Save Our Souls) to other ships, asking for help. One of these ships, the *Carpathia*, started to pick up survivors from the lifeboats at about 8.00 a.m. on 15th April. By the time the *Carpathia* arrived in New York on 19th April, the whole world knew about the tragedy of the *Titanic*. The story of the ship's fate had taken its place in history.

ship called the **********.

Into the Deep

So, what happened to the *Titanic*? Well, it still lies 2.5 miles under the freezing waters of the North Atlantic Ocean … as a rusty wreck! Too deep for most divers, you would have to use a special submarine to reach it. And if you did, you would find clues as to where you were – the grand staircase of the first-class dining room, the hall with fabulous chandeliers, or the famous bow of the once-mighty ship.

QUIZ The Titanic lies under the freezing waters

The watery decks and fish-filled rooms are all that is left of what was once the finest ship on the world's seas. But the tragic story of the Titanic's last night is kept alive in films, documentaries, and books, like the one you have just been reading.

f the Atlantic Ocean as a ★★★★★ wreck.